INCARNADINE

MARY SZYBIST

POEMS

Incarnadine

Also by Mary Szybist
Granted

INCARNADINE

POEMS

Mary Szybist

GRAYWOLF PRESS

This publication is made possible, in part, by the voters of Minnesota through a Minnesota State Arts Board Operating Support grant, thanks to a legislative appropriation from the arts and cultural heritage fund, and through a grant from the National Endowment for the Arts. Significant support has also been provided by Target, the McKnight Foundation, Amazon.com, and other generous contributions from foundations, corporations, and individuals. To these organizations and individuals we offer our heartfelt thanks.

Published by Graywolf Press
250 Third Avenue North, Suite 600
Minneapolis, Minnesota 55401

www.graywolfpress.org

Published in the United States of America

ISBN 978-1-55597-635-4

6 8 10 12 11 9 7 5

Library of Congress Control Number: 2012953979

Cover design: Jeenee Lee Design

Cover art: Botticelli, Sandro (1444–1510). Annunciation. Tempera on wood, 150 × 156 cm. Inv. 1608. Uffizi, Florence, Italy. Photo: Erich Lessing / Art Resource, NY.

Contents

The mysteries of faith are degraded if they are made into an object of affirmation and negation, when in reality they should be an object of contemplation.
—SIMONE WEIL, *GRAVITY AND GRACE*

Repose had again incarnadined her cheeks.
—THOMAS HARDY, *FAR FROM THE MADDING CROWD*

The Troubadours Etc.

Just for this evening, let's not mock them.
Not their curtsies or cross-garters
or ever-recurring pepper trees in their gardens
promising, promising.

At least they had ideas about love.

All day we've driven past cornfields, past cows poking their heads
through metal contraptions to eat.
We've followed West 84, and what else?
Irrigation sprinklers fly past us, huge wooden spools in the fields,
lounging sheep, telephone wires,
yellowing flowering shrubs.

Before us, above us, the clouds swell, layers of them,
the violet underneath of clouds.
Every idea I have is nostalgia. Look up:
there is the sky that passenger pigeons darkened and filled—
darkened for days, eclipsing sun, eclipsing all other sound
with the thunder of their wings.
After a while, it must have seemed that they followed
not instinct or pattern but only
one another.

When they stopped, Audubon observed,
they broke the limbs of stout trees by the weight of the numbers.

And when we stop we'll follow—what?
Our *hearts?*

The Puritans thought that we are granted the ability to love
only through miracle,
but the troubadours knew how to burn themselves through,
how to make themselves shrines to their own longing.
The spectacular was never behind them.

Think of days of those scarlet-breasted, blue-winged birds above you.
Think of me in the garden, humming
quietly to myself in my blue dress,
a blue darker than the sky above us, a blue dark enough for storms,
though cloudless.

At what point is something gone completely?
The last of the sunlight is disappearing
even as it swells—

Just for this evening, won't you put me before you
until I'm far enough away you can
believe in me?

Then try, try to come closer—
my wonderful and less than.

Annunciation (from the grass beneath them)

how many moments did it hover before we felt

it was like nothing else, it was not bird

light as a mosquito, the aroma of walnut husks

while the girl's knees pressed into us

every spear of us rising, sunlit and coarse

the wild bees murmuring through

what did you feel when it was almost upon us when

even the shadows her chin made

never touched but reached just past

the crushed mint, the clover clustered between us

how cool would you say it was

still cool from the clouds

how itchy the air

the girl tilted and lurched and then

we rose up to it, held ourselves tight

when it skimmed just the tips of our blades

didn't you feel softened

no, not even its flickering trembled

Conversion Figure

I spent a long time falling
toward your slender, tremulous face—

a long time slipping through stars
as they shattered, through sticky clouds
with no confetti in them.

I fell toward earth's stony colors
until they brightened, until I could see
the green and white stripes of party umbrellas
propped on your daisied lawn.

From above, you looked small
as an afterthought, something lightly brushed in.
Beside you, blush-pink plates
served up their pillowy cupcakes, and your rosy hems
swirled round your dark head—

I fell and fell.
I fell toward the pulse in your thighs,
toward the cool flamingo of your slip
fluttering past your knees—

Out of God's mouth I fell
like a piece of ripe fruit
toward your deepening shadow.

Girl on the lawn without sleeves, knees bare even of lotion,
time now to strip away everything
you try to think about yourself.

Put down your little dog.
Stop licking the cake from your fingers.

Before today, what darkness
did you let into your flesh? What stillness
did you cast into the soil?

Lift up your head.
Time to enter yourself.
Time to make your own sorrow.

Time to unbrighten and discard
even your slenderness.

Annunciation in *Nabokov* and *Starr*

(*from* The Starr Report *and Nabokov's* Lolita)

I simply can't tell you how gentle, how touching she was.
I knocked, and she opened the door.
She was holding her hem in her hands.

I simply can't tell you how gentle, how calm she was
during her cooperation. In the *windowless hallway,*
I bent toward her.

She was quiet as a cloud.
She touched her mouth with her *damp-smelling hand.*

There was no lake behind us, no *arbor in flame-flower.*
There was a stone wall *the dull white of vague orchards in bloom.*

When she stood up to gather the almost erasable
scents into the damp folds
of her blue dress—

When she *walked through the Rose Garden,*
its heavy, dove-gray air,
dizzy with something unbreathable—

There was something soft and moist about her,
a dare, a rage, an *intolerable tenderness.*

How could I have known
what the sky would do? It was awful to watch
its bright shapes churn and zero
through her, knowing

her body looked like anyone's body
paused at the edge of the garden.

Heroine as She Turns to Face Me

Just before the curtain closes, she turns
toward me, loosening
her gauzy veil & bright hair—

This, she seems to say, *this*
to create scene, the pure sweep of it,
this to give in, feel the lushness,
this & just a little theatrical lighting
& you, too, can be happy,
she's sure of it—

It's as if I cut her heart-whole from the sky,
rag & twist & tongue & the now terrible speed
of her turning

toward me like the spirit
I meant to portray, indefatigable—

see how bravely she turns, how exactly true to the turning,
& in the turning
most herself, as she
arranges herself for the exit

withholding nothing, unraveling
the light in her hair as her face

her bright, unapproachable face
says only that
whatever the next scene is,
she will fill it.

Update on Mary

Mary always thinks that as soon as she gets a few more things done and finishes the dishes, she will open herself to God.

At the gym Mary watches shows about how she should dress herself, so each morning she tries on several combinations of skirts and heels before retreating to her waterproof boots. This takes a long time, so Mary is busy.

Mary can often be observed folding the laundry or watering the plants. It is only when she has a simple, repetitive task that her life feels orderly, and she feels that she is not going to die before she is supposed to die.

Mary wonders if she would be a better person if she did not buy so many almond cookies and pink macaroons.

When people say "Mary," Mary still thinks *Holy Virgin! Holy Heavenly Mother!* But Mary knows she is not any of those things.

Mary worries about not having enough words in her head.

Mary fills her cupboards with many kinds of teas so that she can select from their pastel labels according to her mood: *Tuscan Pear, Earl Grey Lavender, Cherry Rose Green.* But Mary likes only plain red tea and drinks it from morning to night.

Mary has too many silver earrings and likes to sort them in the compartments of her drawer.

Someday Mary would like to think about herself, but she's not yet sure what it means to think, and she's even more confused about herself.

It is not uncommon to find Mary falling asleep on her yoga mat when she has barely begun to stretch.

Mary sometimes closes her eyes and tries to imagine herself as a door swung open. But it is easier to imagine pink macaroons—

Mary likes the solemn titles on her husband's thick books. She feels content and sleepy when he reads them beside her at night—*The Works of Saint Augustine, Critique of Judgment, Paradigm Change in Theology*—but she does not want to read them.

Mary secretly thinks she is pretty and therefore deserves to be loved.

Mary tells herself that if only she could have a child she could carry around like an extra lung, the emptiness inside her would stop gnawing.

It's hard to tell if she believes this.

Mary believes she is a sincere and serious person, but she does not even try to pray.

Some afternoons Mary pretends to read a book, but mostly she watches the patterns of sunlight through the curtains.

On those afternoons, she's like a child who has run out of things to think about.

Mary likes to go out and sit in the yard. If she let herself, she'd stare at the sky all day.

The most interesting things to her are clouds. See, she watches them even by moonlight. Tonight, until bedtime, we can let her have those.

Hail

Mary who mattered to me, gone or asleep
among fruits, spilled

in ash, in dust, I did not

leave you. Even now I can't keep from
composing you, limbs and blue cloak

and soft hands. I sleep to the sound

of your name, I say there is no Mary
except the word Mary, no trace

on the dust of my pillowslip. I only

dream of your ankles brushed by dark violets,
of honeybees above you

murmuring into a crown. Antique queen,

the night dreams on: here are the pears
I have washed for you, here the heavy-winged doves,

asleep by the hyacinths. Here I am,

having bathed carefully in the syllables
of your name, in the air and the sea of them, the sharp scent

of their sea foam. What is the matter with me?

Mary, what word, what dust
can I look behind? I carried you a long way

into my mirror, believing you would carry me

back out. Mary, I am still
for you, I am still a numbness for you.

Annunciation as Fender's Blue Butterfly
with Kincaid's Lupine

*The endangered Fender's blue butterfly associates,
not with common lupines, but with the very rare
Kincaid's lupine.*

—NATIVE PLANT SOCIETY OF OREGON

But if I were this thing,
my mind a thousand times smaller than my wings,

if my fluorescent blue flutter
finally stumbled

into the soft
aqua throats of the blossoms,

if I lost my hunger
for anything else—

I'd do the same. I'd fasten myself
to the touch of the flower.

So what if the milky rims of my wings
no longer stupefied

the sky? If I could
bind myself to this moment, to the slow

snare of its scent,
what would it matter if I became

just the flutter of page
in a text someone turns

to examine me
in the wrong color?

Girls Overheard While Assembling a Puzzle

Are you sure this blue is the same as the
blue over there? This wall's like the
bottom of a pool, its
color I mean. I need a
darker two-piece this summer, the kind with
elastic at the waist so it actually
fits. I can't
find her hands. Where does this gold
go? It's like the angel's giving
her a little piece of honeycomb to eat.
I don't see why God doesn't
just come down and
kiss her himself. This is the red of that
lipstick we saw at the
mall. This piece of her
neck could fit into the light part
of the sky. I think this is a
piece of water. What kind of
queen? You mean
right here? And are we supposed to believe
she can suddenly
talk angel? Who thought this stuff
up? I wish I had a
velvet bikini. That flower's the color of the
veins in my grandmother's hands. I
wish we could
walk into that garden and pick an
X-ray to float on.
Yeah. I do too. I'd say a
zillion yeses to anyone for that.

Invitation

If I can believe in air, I can believe
in the angels of air.

Angels, come breathe with me.

Angel of abortion, angel of alchemy,
angels of barrenness and bliss,
exhale closer. Let me feel
your breath on my teeth—

I call to you, angels of embryos,
earthquakes, you of forgetfulness—

Angels of infection, cover my mouth
and nose with your mouth.

Failed inventions, tilt my head back.

Angels of prostitution and rain,
you of sheerness and sorrow,
you who take nothing,
breathe into me.

You who have cleansed your lips
with fire, I do not need to know
your faces, I do not need you
to have faces.

Angels of water insects, let me sleep
to the sound of your breathing.

You without lungs, make my chest rise—

Without you my air tastes
like nothing. For you
I hold my breath.

Entrances and Exits

In the late afternoon, my friend's daughter walks into my office looking for snacks. She opens the bottom file drawer to take out a bag of rice cakes and a blue carton of rice milk that comes with its own straw. I have been looking at a book of paintings by Duccio. Olivia eats. Bits of puffed rice fall to the carpet.

A few hours ago, the 76-year-old woman, missing for two weeks in the wilderness, was found alive at the bottom of a canyon. The men who found her credit ravens. They noticed ravens circling—

Duccio's *Annunciation* sits open on my desk. The slender angel (dark, green-tipped wings folded behind him) reaches his right hand towards the girl; a vase of lilies sits behind them. But the white dots above the vase don't look like lilies. They look like the bits of puffed rice scattered under my desk. They look like the white fleck at the top of the painting that means both spirit and bird.

Olivia, who is six, picks up the wooden kaleidoscope from my desk and, holding it to her eye, turns it to watch the patterns honeycomb, the colors tumble and change—

Today is the 6th of September. In six days, Russia will hold a day of conception: couples will be given time off from work to procreate, and those who give birth on Russia's national day will receive money, cars, refrigerators, and other prizes.

A six-hour drive from where I sit, deep in the Wallowa Mountains, the woman spent at least six days drifting in and out of consciousness, listening to the swellings of wind, the howls of coyotes, the shaggy-throated ravens—

I turn on the radio. Because he died this morning, Pavarotti's immoderate, unnatural Cs ring out. He said that, singing these notes, he was seized by an animal sensation so intense he would almost lose consciousness.

Duccio's subject is God's entrance into time: time meaning history, meaning a body.

No one knows how the woman survived in her light clothes, what she ate and drank, or what she thought when she looked up into the unkindness of ravens, their loops, their green and purple iridescence flashing—

I think of honeybees. For months, whole colonies have been disappearing from their hives. Where are the bodies? Some blame droughts. Too few flowers, they say: too little nectar.

Consider the ravens. They neither sow nor reap, they have neither storehouse nor barn, and yet God feeds them. (Luke 12:24)

The men never saw the ravens—just heard their deep *caw, caw* circling.

Olivia and I look down on Duccio's scene. I point to the angel's closed lips; she points to his dark wings.

The blue container of rice milk fits loosely into Olivia's hand the same way the book fits into the hand of Duccio's Mary. She punches a hole in the top and, until it is empty, Olivia drinks.

It Is Pretty to Think

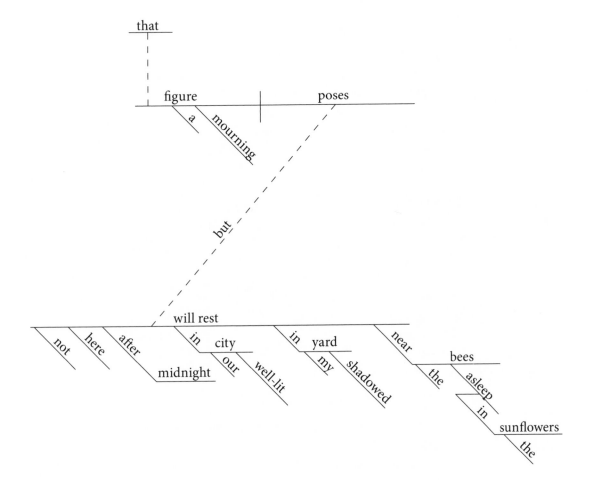

Long after the Desert and Donkey

(Gabriel to Mary)

And of what there would be no end
      —it came quickly.
The wind runs loose, the air churns over us.
No one remembers.

But I remember, under the elm's cool awning,
watching you watch the clouds.
Afternoons passed like afternoons,
and I loved how dull you were.
Given a bit of bark or the buzz
of a bright green fly, you'd smile
for hours. Sweet child, you'd go to anyone.
You had no preferences.

I remember the first time coming toward you,
how solid you looked, sitting and twisting
your dark hair against your neck.

But you were not solid.
From the first moment, when you breathed
on my single lily, I saw
where you felt it.

From then on, I wanted to bend low and close
to the curves of your ear.

There were so many things I wanted to tell you.
Or rather,
I wished to have things that I wanted to tell you.

What a thing, to be with you and have
no words for it. What a thing,
to be outcast like that.

And then everything unfastened.
It was like something was always dissolving
inside you—

Already it's hard to remember
how you used to comb your hair or how you
tilted your broad face in green shade.

Now what seas, what meanings
can I place in you?

Each night, I see you by the window—
sometimes pressing your lips against a pear
you do not eat. Each night,

I see where you feel it:
where there are no mysteries.

To Gabriela at the Donkey Sanctuary

All morning I've thought of you feeding donkeys in the Spanish sun—Donkey Petra, old and full of cancer. Blind Ruby who, you say, loves carrots and takes a long time to eat them. Silver the beautiful horse with the sunken spine who was ridden too young for too long and then abandoned. And the head-butting goat who turned down your delicious kiwi so afterward you wondered why *you* hadn't eaten it.

Here I feed only the unimpressed cats who go out in search of something better. Outside, the solitaires are singing their metallic songs, warning off other birds. Having to come down from the mountain this time of year just to pick at the picked-over trees must craze them a little. I can hear it in their shrill, emphatic notes, a kind of no, no in the undertone.

Gabriela-flown-off-to-save-the-donkeys, it's three hours past dawn. All I've done is read the paper and watch the overcast sky gradually lighten. Breaking news from the West: last night it snowed. A man, drunk, tied a yellow inner-tube to his pickup, whistled in his daughter, and drove in circles, dragging her wildly behind . . .

I know. But to who else can I write of all the things I should not write? I'm afraid I've become one of those childless women who reads too much about the deaths of children. Of the local woman who lured the girl to her house, then cut the baby out of her. Of the mother who threw her children off the bridge, not half a mile from where I sleep.

It's not enough to say the heart wants what it wants. I think of the ravine, the side dark with pines where we lounged through summer days, waiting for something to happen; and of the nights, walking the long way home, the stars so close they seemed to crown us. Once, I asked for your favorite feeling. You said hunger. It felt true then. It was as if we took the bit and bridle from our mouths. From that moment I told myself it was the *not yet* that I wanted, the moving, the toward—

"Be it done unto *me*," we used to say, hoping to be called by the right god. Isn't that why we liked the story of how every two thousand years, a god descends. Leda's pitiless swan. Then Gabriel announcing the new god and his kingdom of lambs—and now? What slouches

toward us? I think I see annunciations everywhere: blackbirds fall out of the sky, trees lift their feathery branches, a girl in an out-sized yellow halo speeds toward—

I picture her last moments, the pickup pulling faster, pulling rougher, kicking up its tracks in the slush: she's nestled into that golden circle, sliding toward the edge of the closed-off field—

I am looking at the postcard of *Anunciación,* the one you sent from Córdoba in the spring. I taped it to the refrigerator next to the grocery list because I wanted to think of you, and because I liked its promise: a world where a girl has only to say yes and heaven opens. But now all I see is a bright innertube pillowing behind her head. All I see is a girl being crushed inside a halo that does not save her.

This is what it's like to be alive without you here: some fall out of the world. I fall back into what I was. Days go by when I do nothing but underline the damp edge of myself.

What I want is what I've always wanted. What I want is to be changed.

Sometimes I half think I'm still a girl beside you—stretched out in the ravine or slouched in the church pews, looking up at the angel and girl in the colored glass, the ruby and sapphire bits lit up inside them. Our scene. All we did was slip from their halos—

Which is to say, *mi corazón,* drink up the sunlight you can and stop feeding the good fruit to the goat. Tell me you believe the world is made of more than all its stupid, stubborn, small refusals, that anything, everything is still possible. I wait for word here where the snow is falling, the solitaires are calling, and I am, as always, your M.

Notes on a 39-Year-Old Body

Most internal organs jiggle and glow and are rosy pink.
The ovary is dull and gray. . . . It is scarred and pitted, for
each cycle of ovulation leaves behind a white blemish where
an egg follicle has been emptied of its contents. The older the
woman, the more scarred her pair of ovaries will be.
    —NATALIE ANGIER, *WOMAN: AN INTIMATE GEOGRAPHY*

She was always planning out her own development,
desiring her own perfection, observing her own progress.
    —HENRY JAMES, *THE PORTRAIT OF A LADY*

in   the   dull

cycle of

desiring

    *

[d]ress[ed]   in

[my] own white

[l]ull

    *

[I]   always plann[ed]   t[o] be

content

    *

Most

foll[y]

[h]old[s]

*

or   is   [s]low

t[o] empt[y]

*

internal   ros[es]   glow

pink   and

red   here

and   [t]her[e]

*

in [s]low

ink

[I]

white[n]

Annunciation under Erasure

And he came to her and said
                    The Lord is

                 troubled
         in   mind

                        be afraid Mary

The Holy
                  will overshadow you
therefore

     be
                nothing   be impossible

And Mary said

And the angel departed from her

Close Reading

But let us return to the words of the poem.
There is more here than a girl on a trampoline,
more than an up-and-down melancholy
movement. Notice, for instance, how far "girl" appears
from the "brandy-colored branches" of the pine.
And notice how close "girl" appears to "silver bar,"
the one that intermittently flashes in the afternoon light.
How she must long for it, separated only by "looks at."
Since this is the work of a humanist poet, we can assume
that when she seems to hear a low whistle,
such as her sister described in line two,
she is really only hearing the high-pitched hum
of her own mind as it unwinds.
This suggests that if she had ever really given herself
to the piano or the violin, she would know
what notes were possible, and therefore
how to make a song of herself.
See all those capital Es in the passage, with their lines
like oven racks placed on the middle rung?
The irony is that this should be a domestic scene, but instead
she is forever bouncing on her trampoline
with the wind in her ears. Though her hands
seem to reach toward that metal bar that hangs
just above and before her, we can't know if she will ever
grasp it. If she does,
she will forfeit her own status as a girl
on a trampoline. Poor girl,
she wants to do what's right, and she knows
that we are watching. We are told
she is concerned about fair play, but consider
how close "fair play" is to "foreplay."
She wants it, but she doesn't know how it goes.
When we direct our gaze at anything,
it collides. She goes on bouncing, and when she tears

the lavender scarf from her neck and says "oh,"
we well might think of "zero." As it floats down
against the backdrop of the endless, dust-colored clouds,
it could only symbolize something terrible as a lung torn from her
in its idle languor earthward.

So-and-So Descending from the Bridge

It is so-and-so and not the dusty world
who drops.

It is their mother and not the dusty world
who drops them.

Why I imagine her so often
empty-handed

as houseboats' distant lights
rise and fall on the far ripples—
I do not know.

I know that darkness.
Have stood on that bridge
in the space between the streetlights
dizzy with looking down.

Maybe some darks are deep enough to swallow
what we want them to.

But you can't have two worlds in your hands
and choose emptiness.

I think that she will never sleep as I sleep,
I who have no so-and-so to throw

or mourn or to let go.

But in that once—with no more
mine, mine, this little so, and that one—

she is what

out-nights me.

So close. So-called

crazy little mother who does not jump.

I Send News: She Has Survived the Tumor after All

To save her, they had to cut her brain in two,
had to sever nerves, strip one lobe almost bare.
It left her blind. Still, she has come through.

Today in her new room she sits and chews
the insides of her cheeks. Her gold scarf glares
on her bald head; her eyes are steelier blue.

Where are you as you read this? There's little news
of war here—something about ambush flares
from TV maps of rivers coursing through

that broken world that soldiers such as you
must now remake. She almost seems to stare
up at the screen. We worry about you.

Not that she'll know you—but she'll know you knew
whatever it was she was. So you'll be air
to her: something borrowed, something blue.

Her mouth hangs quiet, but I don't think she's confused.
She has a face she can't prepare.
She sits and waits with eyes unscrewed.

No need to hurry—but do
come home. Whatever they want of you there,
just finish it. Just do what you must do.
Blind, lobotomized, she waits for you.

Another True Story

The journalist has proof: a photograph of his uncle during the last days of the war, the whole of Florence unfolding behind him, the last standing bridge, the Ponte Vecchio, stretching over the Arno and—you could almost miss it, the point of what is being proved—a small bird on his left shoulder.

Above the rubble, Florence is still Florence. The Duomo is intact, and somewhere in the background, Fra Angelico's winged creatures still descend through their unearthly light, and Da Vinci's calm, soft-featured angel approaches the quiet field—

The war is almost over. The bird has made its choice, and it will remain, perched for days, on his shoulder. And though the captain will soon go home to South Africa and then America and live to be an old man, in this once upon a time in Florence, in 1944, a bird chose him—young, handsome, Jewish, alive—as the one place in the world to rest upon.

When Noah had enough of darkness, he sent forth a dove, but the dove found no ground to rest upon and so returned to him. Later he sent her again, and she returned with an olive branch. The next time she did not return, and so Noah walked back into a world where every burnt offering smelled sweet, and God finally took pity on the imaginations he had made.

Some people took the young captain, walking around for days with that bird on his shoulder, to be a saint, a new Saint Francis, and asked him to bless them, which he did, saying "Ace-King-Queen-Jack," making the sign of the cross.

Saint Good Luck. Saint Young Man who lived through the war. Saint Enough of darkness. Saint Ground for the bird. Saint Say there is a promise here. Saint Infuse the fallen world. Saint How shall this be. Saint Shoulder, Saint Apostrophe, Saint Momentary days. Saint Captain. Saint Covenant of what we cannot say.

Annunciation in *Byrd* and *Bush*

(from Senator Robert Byrd and George W. Bush)

The president goes on. The president goes
on and on, though the senator complains
the language of diplomacy is imbued with courtesy . . .

Who can bear it? I'd rather fasten the words
to a girl, for instance, lounging at the far end of a meadow,
reading her thick book.

I'd rather the president's words were merely spoken by
a stranger who leans in beside her:
you have a decision to make. Either you rise to this moment or . . .

She yawns, silver bracelets clicking
as she stretches her arms—

her cerulean sky studded with green, almost golden pears
hanging from honey-colored branches.

In her blue dress, she's just a bit of that sky,
just a blank bit
fallen into the meadow.

The stranger speaks from the leafy shade.
*Show uncertainty and the world will drift
toward tragedy—*
           Bluster and swagger, she says,
pulling her scarf to her throat as she turns,
impatient to return, to the half-read page—

He steps toward her.
She pulls her bright scarf tight.
For this, he says, *everybody prayed.
A lot of people.* He leans on a branch,
his ear bluish in shadow.

If I say everybody, I don't know if everybody prayed.
I can tell you, a lot prayed.

How still she is.
(Her small lips pursed, her finger still in the pages,
her eyes almost slits as they narrow—)

Nothing matters in this meadow.
There is a girl under pear trees with her book,
and it doesn't matter what she does or does not promise.
There's no next scene to hurt her.
Not even the pears fall down.

I want the words to happen here.
God loves you, and I love you, he says.

Not far beyond his touch,
a wind shakes a dusting of sunlight
onto the edges of pears.

I'd rather think some things are like this.
The water's green edge dissolves
into cerulean, cerulean pearls
into clouds; the girl's unsandaled feet
into uncut fringes of grass—

I don't need to explain, he says
(his sleeves swelling in a nudge of air)

—but the highest call of history,
it changes your heart.

She looks down: her finger in her book.

On a Spring Day in Baltimore, the Art Teacher
Asks the Class to Draw Flowers

I.

I can begin the picture: his neck is bent,
his mouth too close to her ear as he leans in
above her shoulder—to point
to poppies shaded in apricot, stippled
just as he taught her. Class is over.
They are alone in the steady air—

Through the window, a jump rope's tick.
An occasional bird. High voices.
Perhaps, so caught up in composing her flower,
she doesn't feel his fingers
there and there, her neck exposed
to the spring air—

II.

There are only a few lines in the newspaper: her grade, his age, when the police arrived.
J. calls to say he doesn't believe the girl. *Girls that age,* he says—*you know how that goes. Hey, if
there's a trial, you could be a witness.*
  What kind of witness?
  Character witness.

III.

Yes I knew him. One summer we lounged in the backyard sun and listened to songs about what
would be nice. On the swing, on the lawn, I posed for him, leaned my head against the picnic
table. That was when I did not have enough, could not have enough looking at.

That summer he carried his sketchpad everywhere, and on those slow, humid afternoons, I
felt him elongate, shade, and blur. Above us the sky was like a white rush of streetlights, and I
wanted to be nothing but what he shaped in each moment—

I closed my eyes, felt the sunlight on my thighs. To be beheld like that—it felt like glittering.

IV.

What should be remembered, what
imagined?

She shifts in her chair. Her uncertain fingers
trace, against the sky—how many times?—
the red edges of the petals, caress
the darkening lines, trying to still them—
though she cannot make the air stop
breathing, cannot make cannot
make the shuddering lines stay put.

Touch Gallery: Joan of Arc

*The sculptures in this gallery have been
carefully treated with a protective wax
so that visitors may touch them.*

—EXHIBITIONS, THE ART INSTITUTE
OF CHICAGO

Stone soldier, it's okay now.
I've removed my rings, my watch, my bracelets.

I'm allowed, brave girl,
to touch you here, where the mail covers your throat,
your full neck, down your shoulders
to here, where raised unlatchable buckles
mock-fasten your plated armor.

Nothing peels from you.

Your skin gleams like the silver earrings
you do not wear.

Above you, museum windows gleam October.
Above you, high gold leaves flinch in the garden,

but the flat immovable leaves entwined in your hair to crown you
go through what my fingers can't.
I want you to have a mind I can turn in my hands.

You have a smooth and upturned chin,
cold cheeks, unbruisable eyes,
and hair as grooved as fig skin.

It's October, but it's not October
behind your ears, which don't hint
of dark birds moving overhead,
or of the blush and canary leaves

emptying themselves
in slow spasms
into shallow hedgerows.

Still bride of your own armor,
bride of your own blind eyes,
this isn't an appeal.

If I could I would let your hair down
and make your ears disappear.

Your head at my shoulder, my fingers on your lips—

as if the cool of your stone curls were the cool
      of an evening—
as if you were about to eat salt from my hand.

To the Dove within the Stone

Sleeper, still untouched by
gravity, invisible
for the stone, I cannot

hear you shift in its dark
center. How many centuries
since the first girl—pressing hand

against stone—hardly meaning to
make an inside—
roused you? The stone had no

emptiness, and her body no
emptiness until she felt you
move under her palm, her steady

pulse. Already flesh was something to
stir you, something to make you
true. Stone-dove, untouched

by thistles, moths,
listen now
my hand is open.

Holy

Spirit who knows me, I do not feel you
fall so far in me,

do not feel you turn in my dark center.

My mother is sick, and you
cannot help her.

My beautiful, moon-faced mother is sick
and you sleep in the dark edges of her shadow.

Spirit made to
know me, is this your weight
in my throat, my
chest, the breath heavy so I hardly
breathe it?

I do not believe in the beauty of falling.

Over and over in the dark I tell myself
I do not have to believe
in the beauty of falling

though she edges toward you,
saying your name with such steadiness.

I sit winding blue tape around my wrists
to keep my hands from falling.

Holy Ghost, I come for you today
in this overlit afternoon as she

picks at the bread with her small hands,
her small rough hands,
the wide blue veins that have always been her veins
winding through them.

Ghost, what am I
if I lose the one
who's always known me?

Spirit, know me.

Shadow, are you here
splintering into the bread's thick crust as it
crumbles into my palms, is that
you, the dry cough in her lungs, the blue tape on my wrists.
The dark hair that used to fall over her shoulders.

Fragile mother, impossible spirit, will you fall so far
from me, will you leave me
to me?

To think it
is the last hard kiss, that seasick

silence, your bits of breath

diffusing in my mouth—

How (Not) to Speak of God

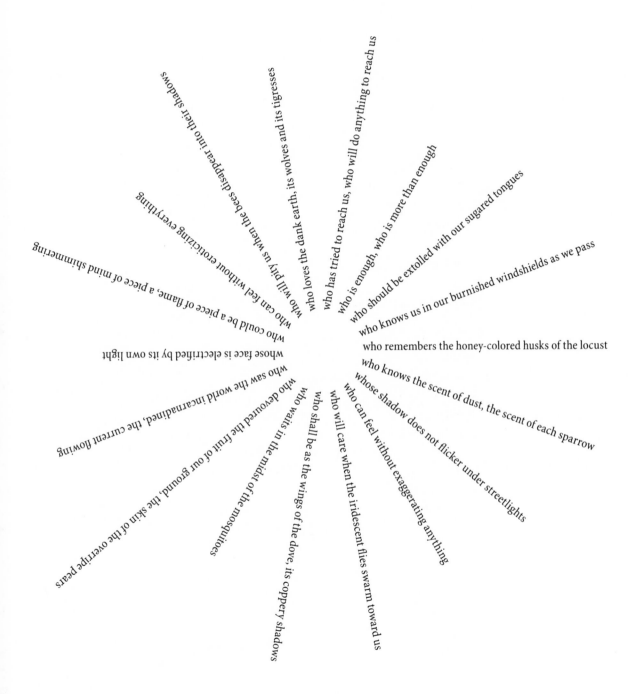

who has tried to reach us, who will do anything to reach us

who is enough, who is more than enough

who should be extolled with our sugared tongues

who knows us in our burnished windshields as we pass

who remembers the honey-colored husks of the locust

who knows the scent of dust, the scent of each sparrow

whose shadow does not flicker under streetlights

who can feel without exaggerating anything

who shall be as the wings of the dove, its coppery shadows

who will care when the iridescent flies swarm toward us

who waits in the midst of the mosquitoes

who devoured the fruit of our ground, the skin of the overripe pears

who saw the world incarnadined, the current flowing

whose face is electrified by its own light

who could be a piece of flame, a piece of mind shimmering

who can feel without eroticizing everything

who will pity us when the bees disappear into their shadows

who loves the dank earth, its wolves and its tigresses

Yet Not Consumed

But give me the frost of your name
in my mouth, give me
spiny fruits and scaly husks—
give me breath

to say aloud to the breathless clouds
your name, to say
I am, let me need
to say it and still need you
to give me need, to make me
into what is needed, what you need, no

more than that I am, no more
than the stray wind on my neck, the salt
of your palm on my tongue, no more

than need, a neck that will bend
lower to what I am, so
give me creeping, give me clouds that hang
low and sweep the blue of the sky
to its edges, let me taste the edges, the bread-colored clouds,
here I am, give me

thumb and fingers, give me only
what I need, a turn here
to turn what I am
into I am, what your name writ in clouds
writ on me

On Wanting to Tell [   ] about a Girl Eating Fish Eyes

—how her loose curls float
above the silver fish as she leans in
to pluck its eyes.

You died just hours ago.
Not suddenly, no. You'd been dying so long
nothing looked like itself: from your window,
fishermen swirled sequins;
fishnets entangled the moon.

Now the dark rain
looks like dark rain. Only the wine
shimmers with candlelight. I refill the glasses
as we raise a toast to you
as so-and-so's daughter—elfin, jittery as a sparrow—
slides into another lap
to eat another pair of slippery eyes
with her soft fingers, fingers rosier each time,
for being chewed a little.

If only I could go to you, revive you.
You must be a little alive still.
I'd like to put the girl in your lap.
She's almost feverishly warm, and she weighs
hardly anything. I want to show you how
she relishes each eye, to show you
her greed for them.

She is placing one on her tongue,
bright as a polished coin—

What do they taste like? I ask.
Twisting in my lap, she leans back sleepily.
They taste like eyes, she says.

Annunciation in Play

—into the 3rd second, the girl
holds on, determined not to meet his gaze—

she swerves her blue sleeve,
closes down the space,
while his eyes are intent, unwilling
to relent and

late into the 5th second they are still
fighting on, their feet sinking into
the slippery grass—

Approaching the 6th second
he can't repeat the sweeping in
and each time he tries to clear
the way to her thorn-brown eyes by the gesture of a hand
it is easily blocked by the turn
of her cheek.

By the 8th second she is still repelling
every attempt, still deflecting (you can see
the speed, the skillful knee action)
his gaze. And she must know (she has to think
every second, there's no letting up)
this is only
delay, but the delay

is what she has
before his expert touch
swings in, before
she loses her light, clean edges, before she
loses possession—

before they look at each other.

Too Many Pigeons to Count and One Dove

Bellagio, Italy

—3:21   The startled ash tree
                    alive with them, wings lacing
          through silver-green leaves—jumping

—3:24   from branch to branch
          they rattle the leaves, or make the green leaves
                    sound dry—

—3:26   The surprise of a boat horn from below.
               Increasingly voluptuous
            fluttering.

—3:28   One just there on the low branch—
                    gone before I can breathe or
               describe it.

—3:29   Nothing stays long enough to know.
          How long since we've been inside
                    anything together the way

—3:29   these birds are inside
          this tree together, shifting, making it into
                    a shivering thing?

—3:30   A churchbell rings once.
               One pigeon flies
          over the top of the tree without skimming

—3:30   the high leaves, another
          flies to the tree below. I cannot find
               a picture of you in my mind

—3:30   to land on. In the overlapping of soft dark
               leaves, wings look
                    to be tangled, but

—3:32   I see when they pull apart, one bird far, one
near, they did not touch. One bird seems caught,
         flapping violently, one

—3:32   becomes still and tilts down—
             I cannot find the dove,
        have not seen it for minutes. One pigeon nips

—3:32   at something on a high branch,
moves lower (it has taken this long for me to understand
          that they are eating). Two flap

—3:33   their wings without leaving their branches and
           I am tired
        of paying attention. The birds are all the same

—3:33   to me. It's too warm to stay still in the sun, leaning
      over this wood fence to try to get a better look
       into the branches. Why

—3:33   do the pigeons gather in this tree
       or that one, why leave one for another
in this moment or that one, why do I miss you

—3:33   now, but not now,
      my old idea of you, the feeling for you I lost
and remade so many times until it was

—3:33   something else, as strange as your touch
        was familiar. Why not look up
at high white Alps or down at the

—3:33   untrumpeted shadows bronzing the water
        or wonder why an almost lavender smoke
       hovers over that particular orange villa

—3:33   on the far shoreline or if I am
                              capable of loving you better
                    or at all from this distance.

The Cathars Etc.

loved the spirit most
so to remind them of the ways of the flesh,
those of the old god

took one hundred prisoners and cut off
each nose
each pair of lips

and scooped out each eye

until just one eye on one man was left
to lead them home.

People did that, I say to myself,

a human hand lopping at a man's nose
over and over with a dull blade

that could not then slice
the lips clean
but like an old can opener, pushed
into skin, sawed
the soft edges, working each lip

slowly off as
both men heavily, intimately
breathed.

My brave believer, in my private re-enactments,
you are one of them.

I pick up in the aftermath where you're being led
by rope
by the one with the one good eye.

I'm one of the women at the edge of the hill
watching you stagger magnificently,
unsteadily back.

All your faces are tender with holes
starting to darken and scab

and I don't understand how you could
believe in anything that much
that is not me.

The man with the eye pulls you
forward. You're in the square now.
The women are hysterical,
the men are making terrible sounds
from unclosable mouths.

And I don't know if I can do it, if I can touch
a lipless face that might
lean down, instinctively,
to try to kiss me.

White rays are falling through the clouds.
You are holding that imbecile rope.
You are waiting to be claimed.

What do I love more than this
image of myself?

There I am in the square walking toward you
calling you out by name.

To You Again

Again this morning my eyes woke up too close
to your eyes,

their almost green orbs
too heavy-lidded to really look back.

To wake up next to you
is ordinary. I do not even need to look at you

to see you.
But I do look. So when you come to me

in your opulent sadness, I see
you do not want me

to unbutton you
so I cannot do the one thing

I can do.
Now it is almost one a.m. I am still at my desk

and you are upstairs at your desk a staircase
away from me. Already it is years

of you a staircase
away from me. To be near you

and not near you
is ordinary.

You
are ordinary.

Still, how many afternoons have I spent
peeling blue paint from

our porch steps, peering above
hedgerows, the few parked cars for the first

glimpse of you. How many hours under
the overgrown, pink camillas, thinking

the color was wrong for you, thinking
you'd appear

after my next
blink.

Soon you'll come down the stairs
to tell me something. And I'll say,

okay. Okay. I'll say it
like that, say it just like

that, I'll go on being
your never-enough.

It's not the best in you
I long for. It's when you're noteless,

numb at the ends of my fingers, all is
all. I say it is.

Annunciation: Eve to Ave

The wings behind the man I never saw.
But often, afterward, I dreamed his lips,
remembered the slight angle of his hips,
his feet among the tulips and the straw.

I liked the way his voice deepened as he called.
As for the words, I liked the showmanship
with which he spoke them. Behind him, distant ships
went still; the water was smooth as his jaw—

And when I learned that he was not a man—
bullwhip, horsewhip, unzip, I could have crawled
through thorn and bee, the thick of hive, rosehip,
courtship, lordship, gossip and lavender.
(But I was quiet, quiet as
eagerness—that astonished, dutiful fall.)

Annunciation Overheard from the Kitchen

I could hear them from the kitchen, speaking as if
something important had happened.

I was washing the pears in cool water, cutting
the bruises from them.
From my place at the sink, I could hear

a jet buzz hazily overhead, a vacuum
start up next door, the click,
click between shots.

"Mary, step back from the camera."

There was a softness to his voice
but no fondness, no hurry in it.

There were faint sounds
like walnuts being dropped by crows onto the street,
almost a brush
of windchime from the porch—

Windows around me everywhere half-open—

My skin alive with the pitch.

Night Shifts at the Group Home

for Lily Mae

The job was easy: I tucked
them in, kicked off my shoes, listened for
the floor to go quiet. Everyone

slept except one: outside her door,
she paced, she hummed, holding
the edge of her torn

nightgown. Pointing, I told
her: to bed. *Your* bed. But she would not
stay there. She was old,

older than my mother: manic, caught
up in gibberish, determined to
sleep on my cot—

At first it was just to
quiet her. I could only sleep
if she slept, and I needed relief

from myself. That is how she
became a body next to mine
whether or not I wanted there to be

a body. She climbed
into my bed. I let her
sleep hot and damp against my spine.

All night she rocked, she turned,
she poked her spastic elbows
into my calves and slurred

her broken noises in the dark. All the old
fans went round in clicks
those summer nights—and she rolled

in bed and kicked
me in the head and I was
happy. No words, no tricks,

I just didn't love
my loneliness. My mind
felt cooler

with her there. Beside
her, I could have been anyone.
She had no word for me and not the kind

of mind to keep one.
And if she kicked
me, some nights, just

for the fun of it—who was I
to disappoint my one?
Sometimes I imagine I

was someone she won
at a fair as the wheel spun
under the floating, unfaltering sun

and clicked each lucky one
and one
until I was happily undone.

Happy Ideas

I had the happy idea to fasten a bicycle wheel
to a kitchen stool and watch it turn.

—DUCHAMP

I had the happy idea to suspend some blue globes in the air

and watch them pop.

I had the happy idea to put my little copper horse on the shelf so we could stare at each other all evening.

I had the happy idea to create a void in myself.

Then to call it natural.

Then to call it supernatural.

I had the happy idea to wrap a blue scarf around my head and spin.

I had the happy idea that somewhere a child was being born who was nothing like Helen or Jesus except in the sense of changing everything.

I had the happy idea that someday I would find both pleasure and punishment, that I would know them and feel them,

and that, until I did, it would be almost as good to pretend.

I had the happy idea to call myself happy.

I had the happy idea that the dog digging a hole in the yard in the twilight had his nose deep in mold-life.

I had the happy idea that what I do not understand is more real than what I do,

and then the happier idea to buckle myself

into two blue velvet shoes.

I had the happy idea to polish the reflecting glass and say

hello to my own blue soul. *Hello, blue soul. Hello.*

It was my happiest idea.

Annunciation as Right Whale with Kelp Gulls

The gulls have learned to feed on the whales. . . .
The proportion of whales attacked annually has
soared from 1% in 1974 to 78% today.

—BBC NEWS

I tell you I have seen them in their glee

diving fast into the sureness of her flesh,
fast into the softness of

her wounds—have seen them

peel her, have seen them give themselves

full to the effort and the
lull of it—

        Why wouldn't such sweetness
be for them?

For they outnumber her.

For she is tender, pockmarked, full

of openness. For they

swoop down on her wherever she surfaces. For they

eat her alive. For they take mercy on others and show them the way.

At high tide, more gulls lift from the mussel beds and soar toward her.

For they do sit and eat, for they do sit and eat

a sweetness prepared for them

until she disappears again into the water.

Here, There Are Blueberries

When I see the bright clouds, a sky empty of moon and stars,
I wonder what I am, that anyone should note me.

Here there are blueberries, what should I fear?
Here there is bread in thick slices, of whom should I be afraid?

Under the swelling clouds, we spread our blankets.
Here in this meadow, we open our baskets

to unpack blueberries, whole bowls of them,
berries not by the work of our hands, berries not by the work of our fingers.

What taste the bright world has, whole fields
without wires, the blackened moss, the clouds

swelling at the edges of the meadow. And for this,
I did nothing, not even wonder.

You must live for something, they say.
People don't live just to keep on living.

But here is the quince tree, a sky bright and empty.
Here there are blueberries, there is no need to note me.

Do Not Desire Me, Imagine Me

As Corpse   Loosened, bare, profusely female,
          the pulse in my thigh
          unthreaded—

As Hair   Clear of furies, of flowers,
          the shade of dry paste

As Skull   Fissured:
          an unlit chandelier

As Dirt   The ants sift through
          and soften

          And with no fingertips, imagine

As Dust   You can hang the air on me

Insertion of Meadow with Flowers

In 1371, beneath the angel's feet,

Veneziano added a meadow—
a green expanse with white
and yellow broom flowers, the kind
that—until the sun warms them—
have no scent—

God could have chosen other means than flesh.

Imagine he did
and the girl on her knees in this meadow—
open, expectant, dreamily rocking,
her mouth open, quiet—

is only important because we recognize

the wish. For look, the flowers
do not spin, not even

the threads of their shadows—
and they are infused
with what they did not
reach for.

Out of nothing does not mean

into nothing.

Knocking or Nothing

Knock me or nothing, the things of this world
ring in me, shrill-gorged and shrewish,

clicking their charms and their chains and their spouts.
Let them. Let the fans whirr.

All the similar virgins must have emptied
their flimsy pockets, and I

was empty enough,
sugared and stretched on the unmown lawn,

dumb as the frost-pink tongues
of the unpruned roses.

When you put your arms around me in that moment,
when you pulled me to you and leaned

back, when you lifted me
just a few inches, when you shook me

hard then, had you ever heard
such emptiness?

I had room for every girl's locket,
every last dime and pocketknife.

Oh my out-sung, fierce, unthinkable—
why rattle only the world

you placed in me? Won't you clutter the unkissed,
idiot stars? They blink and blink

like quiet shepherds,
like brides-about-your-neck.

Call them out of that quietness.
Knock them in their nothing, against their empty enamel,

against the dark that has no way to hold them
and no appetite.

Call in the dead to touch them.
Let them slip on their own chinks of light.

The Lushness of It

It's not that the octopus wouldn't love you—
not that it wouldn't reach for you
with each of its tapering arms.

You'd be as good as anyone, I think,
to an octopus. But the creatures of the sea,
like the sea, don't think

about themselves, or you. Keep on floating there,
cradled, unable to burn. Abandon
yourself to the sway, the ruffled eddies, abandon

your heavy legs to the floating meadows
      of seaweed and feel
            the bloom of phytoplankton, spindrift, sea
        spray, barnacles. In the dark benthic realm, the slippery nekton
glide over the abyssal plains and as you float you can feel
              that upwelling of cold, deep water touch
      the skin stretched over
          your spine. No, it's not that the octopus
            wouldn't love you. If it touched,

if it tasted you, each of its three
hearts would turn red.

Will theologians of any confession refute me?
Not the bluecap salmon. Not its dotted head.

Notes

And in the sixth month the angel Gabriel was sent from God unto a city of Galilee, named Nazareth, to a virgin espoused to a man whose name was Joseph, of the house of David; and the virgin's name was Mary. And the angel came in unto her, and said, Hail, thou that art highly favoured, the Lord is with thee: blessed art thou among women. And when she saw him, she was troubled at his saying, and cast in her mind what manner of salutation this should be. And the angel said unto her, Fear not, Mary: for thou hast found favour with God. And, behold, thou shalt conceive in thy womb, and bring forth a son, and shalt call his name JESUS. He shall be great, and shall be called the Son of the Highest: and the Lord God shall give unto him the throne of his father David: And he shall reign over the house of Jacob for ever; and of his kingdom there shall be no end. Then said Mary unto the angel, How shall this be, seeing I know not a man? And the angel answered and said unto her, The Holy Ghost shall come upon thee, and the power of the Highest shall overshadow thee: therefore also that holy thing which shall be born of thee shall be called the Son of God. And, behold, thy cousin Elisabeth, she hath also conceived a son in her old age: and this is the sixth month with her, who was called barren. For with God nothing shall be impossible. And Mary said, Behold the handmaid of the Lord; be it unto me according to thy word. And the angel departed from her.—King James Bible, Luke 1:26–38

"Annunciation in *Nabokov* and *Starr*": Italicized phrases in this poem are taken from *Lolita* by Vladimir Nabokov and *The Starr Report* by Kenneth Starr.

"It Is Pretty to Think" is inspired by grade-school diagrams by my mother-in-law, Helen White. Thank you, Helen, for sharing your school notebooks.

"To Gabriela at the Donkey Sanctuary" is inspired in part by Lucie Brock-Broido's poem "Ten Years Apprenticeship" from *A Hunger*. This poem is for Gabriela Rife.

"Notes on a 39-Year-Old Body": The language of each section is taken from the combined text of the two epigraphs. Imported language is marked in brackets.

"So-and-So Descending from the Bridge": A mother threw her two children off the Sellwood Bridge in Portland, Oregon, in the early morning hours of May 23, 2009. One child died; one survived.

"Another True Story": Thank you to Roger Cohen for sharing the photograph and for relating Bert Cohen's story so powerfully in the essay "Lake Water Reflections." The essay, in adapted form, will appear in his forthcoming family memoir, *The Girl from Human Street*.

"Annunciation in *Byrd* and *Bush*": Italicized phrases in this poem, words of Senator Robert Byrd and President George W. Bush, are taken from various sources including:

George W. Bush's Address to a Joint Session of Congress, September 20, 2001, and "Remarks by the President to Coal Miners and Their Families and Their Community," Green Tree Fire Department, Green Tree, Pennsylvania, 2002.

Senator Robert Byrd's remarks to the Senate on February 13, 2003 (Congressional Record 108th Congress).

"Holy" is for my mother, Carla Gerber Szybist (June 19, 1940–August 3, 2013).

"How (Not) to Speak of God": The title is taken from Peter Rollins's book of the same name.

"Yet Not Consumed": "And the angel of the Lord appeared to him in a flame of fire out of the midst of a bush. He looked, and behold, the bush was burning, yet it was not consumed." —Exodus 3:2

"On Wanting to Tell [   ] about a Girl Eating Fish Eyes": "Your Majesty, when we compare the present life of man with that time of which we have no knowledge, it seems to me like the swift flight of a lone sparrow through the banqueting-hall where you sit in the winter months to dine with your thanes and counselors. Inside there is a comforting fire to warm the room; outside, the wintry storms of snow and rain are raging. This sparrow flies swiftly in through one door of the hall, and out through another. While he is inside, he is safe from the wintry storms; but after a few moments of comfort, he vanishes from sight into the darkness whence he came. Similarly, man appears on earth for a little while, but we know nothing of what went before this life, and what follows." —Bede, *A History of the English Church and People.* This poem is for Donald Justice.

"The Cathars Etc.": "Here at the isolated Lastours castles, which were built along a defensive cliff spur, the Cathars spent much of 1209 heroically fending off the onslaught. So the crusader leader, the sadistic Simon de Montfort, resorted to primitive psychological warfare. He ordered his troops to gouge out the eyes of 100 luckless prisoners, cut off their noses and lips, then send them back to the towers led by a prisoner with one remaining eye." —"The Besieged and the Beautiful in Languedoc" by Tony Perrottet, *The New York Times,* May 6, 2010.

"Happy Ideas": "And why that cerulean color? The blue comes partly from the sea, partly from the sky. While water in a glass is transparent, it absorbs slightly more red light than blue . . . the red light is absorbed out and what gets reflected back to space is mainly blue." —Carl Sagan, *Pale Blue Dot*

"Here, There Are Blueberries": The italicized phrases are adapted from Anat Cohen, as quoted by Jeffrey Goldberg in his 2004 *New Yorker* article, "Among the Settlers": "You don't live just to keep living. That's not the point of life." This poem is for my father, Charles A. Szybist.

Acknowledgments

Sincere thanks to the editors of the following journals in which these poems first appeared, sometimes in different forms:

Agni Online: "Do Not Desire Me, Imagine Me." *The Burnside Review:* "The Heroine as She Turns to Face Me." *The Cincinnati Review*: "Annunciation as Fender's Blue Butterfly with Kincaid's Lupine." *The Chronicle of Higher Education Review*: "Happy Ideas." *Electronic Poetry Review*: "The Lushness of It" and "Invitation." *Fifth Wednesday Journal*: "Night Shifts at the Group Home." *The Iowa Review*: "Annunciation (from the grass beneath them)," "Annunciation under Erasure," "Annunciation in Play," and "Annunciation: Eve to Ave." *The Kenyon Review*: "Yet Not Consumed," "Girls Overheard While Assembling a Puzzle," "Annunciation as Right Whale with Kelp Gulls," and "On a Spring Day in Baltimore, the Art Teacher Asks the Class to Grow Flowers." *The Laurel Review*: "You Tell Me to Take a—" (now titled "Holy"). *Lo-Ball*: "Annunciation Overheard from the Kitchen." *Long Journey: Contemporary Northwest Poets Anthology*: "Knocking or Nothing" and "*Touch Gallery*: Joan of Arc." *Meridian*: "The Troubadours Etc." and "Close Reading." *Ploughshares*: "Here, There Are Blueberries" and "So-and-So Descending from the Bridge." *Plume*: "Notes on a 39-Year-Old Body." *Poetry*: "On Wanting to Tell [   ] about a Girl Eating Fish Eyes" and "Hail." *Poets.org, The Academy of American Poets Poem-a-Day Series*: "All Times & All Tenses Alive in This Moment" (now titled "How (Not) to Speak of God"). *Sou'wester*: "Entrances and Exits." *Tin House*: "Annunciation in *Byrd* and *Bush*," "Annunciation in *Nabokov* and *Starr*." *The Virginia Quarterly Review*: "I Send News: She Has Survived the Tumor after All." *West Branch*: "Insertion of Meadow with Flowers" and "Long after the Desert and Donkey." *Witness*: "Conversion Figure."

"How (Not) to Speak of God" (originally titled "All Times & All Tenses Alive in This Moment") can be viewed on the ceiling of the portico of the Pennsylvania College of Arts & Design, where it was painted as a mural by the artist team Root 222 as part of *Poetry Paths*, a public visual and literary art project in the city of Lancaster, Pennsylvania.

"The Troubadours Etc." also appeared in *The Best American Poetry 2008*, edited by Charles Wright and David Lehman.

"The Troubadours Etc.," "The Lushness of It," and "Annunciation as Fender's Blue Butterfly with Kincaid's Lupine" also appeared in *The Autumn House Anthology of Contemporary Poetry, Second Edition*.

"On a Spring Day in Baltimore, the Art Teacher Asks the Class to Draw Flowers" also appeared in *Pushcart Prize Anthology XXVII*.

"Annunciation: Eve to Ave," "Annunciation (from the grass beneath them)," and "Girls Overheard While Assembling a Puzzle" also appeared on *Poetry Daily*.

"To the Dove within the Stone": This poem appeared as part of the *Manual Labors* exhibit at the Laboratory of Art and Ideas at Belmar in Denver, Colorado.

Thank you to William Olsen for selecting "Night Shifts at the Group Home" as the winner of the *Fifth Wednesday Journal* Editor's Prize in Poetry for 2012.

I am grateful to Lewis & Clark College, the MacDowell Colony, the National Endowment for the Arts, the Witter Bynner Foundation (and to Kay Ryan for selecting me for a fellowship), and the Rockefeller Foundation Bellagio Center for generous fellowships and support that enabled me to complete this collection.

Thank you Gabriela Rife, archangel and muse to this collection. The heroine of "Entrances and Exits" and "On Wanting to Tell [   ] about a Girl Eating Fish Eyes" is Olivia Glosser Asher. Thank you, Olivia. Thank you, Michele Glazer, for going a long way into these poems with me and helping me through them. I am grateful to many readers for their attention, care, and invaluable help, especially Endi Bogue Hartigan, Molly Lou Freeman, Mark Szybist, D. A. Powell, John Casteen, Joy Katz, Rachel Cole, Katie Ford, Sara Guest, and Jeffrey Shotts. Thank you to my husband, Jerry Harp, for always helping me see the potential in my attempts, and for believing in them. To my colleagues, friends, and family, my deepest gratitude for your generosity, support, and friendship.

MARY SZYBIST is the author of a previous collection of poems, *Granted,* which was named a finalist for the National Book Critics Circle Award. The recipient of a fellowship from the National Endowment for the Arts, a Rona Jaffe Foundation Writing Award, and a Witter Bynner Fellowship from the Library of Congress, she lives in Portland, Oregon, and teaches at Lewis & Clark College and the Warren Wilson MFA Program for Writers.

The text of *Incarnadine* is set in Minion Pro, an original typeface designed by Robert Slimbach in 1990. Composition by BookMobile Design and Digital Publisher Services, Minneapolis, Minnesota. Manufactured by Versa Press on acid-free 30 percent postconsumer wastepaper.